LION'S DEN SURVIVAL PRINCIPLES
For media professionals . . . and everyone else

By Larry W. Poland

DEDICATION

To Frank J. Poland, my dearly-loved father,
whose godly wisdom
stood him in good stead for ninety-six years,
and me for sixty-nine,
until he departed for a far better place
July 16, 2008.

INTRODUCTION

Living life successfully isn't easy . . . or difficult. It is impossible!

There is one part of this fact that God utilizes. We are such arrogant creatures, that if living successfully were, at any level, achievable through human effort, we'd pound our chests and boast of our success. I know this is true, because that is exactly what we do so long as life goes well for us.

But, it is in our struggles, conflicts, and adversity that we often fulfill God's plan for our lives—turning to Him for help and, in the process, building a deep and intimate relationship with the Maker we typically ignore while things are going well. It is when we get painted into a corner that the only way *out* is *up*.

No human being understood this dynamic more than the Hebrew prophet Daniel. Captured and taken as a slave with some of his teenaged friends to Nebuchadnezzar's Babylon, life was not pleasant. In that great city of the ancient world, Daniel faced a ruthless regime hostile to his people and his faith. But, in nonnegotiable reliance on the God of Abraham, the True and Living God, he conquered his circumstances, survived three regime changes, and was still serving Jehovah in his eighties. Lesser men succumbed to their captors and their pagan ways. Daniel created a legacy that is proverbial the world around. Betrayed by his jealous peers in the kingdom in which he served as vizier or prime minister, Daniel ended up on "death row." "Daniel in the lion's den" is a story of divine deliverance that thrills the most blasé and challenges the faithless to explore the One who shut the lion's mouths.

Lion's Den . . .

There are many environments in contemporary life which are hostile to people of deep faith, especially the biblical Christian faith. Often mocked in the culture, ridiculed in the work place, lampooned and slandered in TV sitcoms, portrayed in damning ways in films, and hated and slaughtered by Jihadists, devout followers of Jesus Christ are increasingly marginalized by society.

This is not new. Ask any Jewish person who has been— or is now—the object of scorn, violence, and even plots for torture or annihilation. Daniel is one of millions of Jews over the centuries who understands "being thrown to the lions" as the result of an evil conspiracy. Interesting, isn't it, that believers in Jehovah—both Christians and Jews— get such treatment.

Survival Principles . . .

There is a way to survive in hostile—even life-threatening—situations. In this book, we learn from the masters. Babylonian culture was so contemptuous of the faith of Daniel, Hananiah, Mishael and Azariah that their masters forced them to give up their names that honored Jehovah and take names honoring pagan deities— Belteshazzar, Shadrach, Meshach, and Abednego. Then, the whip, the scimitar, the fiery furnace, or the lion's den awaited . . . upon any evidence of religious nonconformity.

But, in violation of "conventional wisdom" from the culture, these brave men staked their faith in the deliverance of their God—if not deliverance here and now, in the life hereafter. Either way, they survived.

For Media Professionals . . .

One of America's most hostile environments for unflinching followers of Jesus Christ is the entertainment industry. Having served since 1980 in this industry in both Hollywood and New York, I can tell you honestly that the people who run entertainment are often bitter enemies of the Christian faith and of Christians, especially evangelicals. "Jesus Christ!" is a commonly used expletive.

This book's content was originally written for the Christian Faithful working in media. It was a column in a publication by Mastermedia International named *The Median*. It was well received. A major market news anchor whom I had never before met told me how the column had sustained her in her faith for years during some tempestuous times in her personal life and career.

. . . And Everyone Else.

When believers *outside of media* began writing with words of gratitude and requesting permission to reprint individual columns or the entire series in their publications, I felt I should make it available to the Christian community at large.

So, pretend that you work for a film studio, a television network, an Internet company, or a print media corporation. Or, just "look over the shoulder" of those who do work in media and learn from the timeless, divine principles that have helped them survive.

Sooner or later, you'll face your own "fiery furnace" or be "thrown to the lions."

Survive . . . and Conquer!

As you rely on God for deliverance, you will face lions that look much like the one portrayed throughout this book. That doleful look is of a hungry beast that—for reasons he does not understand—cannot get his teeth into you or his jaws around you. Something has given him "lockjaw." Better . . . someONE has given him lockjaw.

TABLE OF CONTENTS

LION'S DEN SURVIVAL PRINCIPLES, PART 1
Defining Your Nonnegotiables and Counting the Cost 13

LION'S DEN SURVIVAL PRINCIPLES, PART 2
Making a Living vs. Making a Life 17

LION'S DEN SURVIVAL PRINCIPLES, PART 3
Watching Out for the Tiny Compromises 21

LION'S DEN SURVIVAL PRINCIPLES, PART 4
Praying *Before* all Else Has Failed 25

LION'S DEN SURVIVAL PRINCIPLES, PART 5
Hanging in There Until Your Big Break Comes 29

LION'S DEN SURVIVAL PRINCIPLES, PART 6
Establishing the Fact That You Can't Be "Bought" 33

LION'S DEN SURVIVAL PRINCIPLES, PART 7
Dealing with the Power Structure 37

LION'S DEN SURVIVAL PRINCIPLES, PART 8
How to Frustrate Your Enemies 41

LION'S DEN SURVIVAL PRINCIPLES, PART 9
Obedience Over Consequence 45

LION'S DEN SURVIVAL PRINCIPLES, PART 10
A Spirit That Sets You Apart 49

LION'S DEN SURVIVAL PRINCIPLES, PART 11
Giving Credit Where Credit Is Due 53

LION'S DEN SURVIVAL PRINCIPLES, PART 12
How to Weather Adversity 55

LION'S DEN SURVIVAL PRINCIPLES, PART 13
Surviving the Fire 57

LION'S DEN SURVIVAL PRINCIPLES, PART 14
How to Get Demoted 61

LION'S DEN SURVIVAL PRINCIPLES, PART 15
Identifying With the Sins of Your Community 65

LION'S DEN SURVIVAL PRINCIPLES, PART 16
Discovering the Power of Praise Over Problems 69

LION'S DEN SURVIVAL PRINCIPLES, PART 17
Waiting Until the "Last Chapter" is Written 73

LION'S DEN SURVIVAL PRINCIPLES, PART 18
Getting Past Ego to Reach Understanding 77

LION'S DEN SURVIVAL PRINCIPLES, PART 19
How to Acquire Good References 79

LION'S DEN SURVIVAL PRINCIPLES, PART 20
How to Pray And Be Heard 81

LION'S DEN SURVIVAL PRINCIPLES, PART 21
Letting God Have Your Enemies for Lunch 85

LION'S DEN SURVIVAL PRINCIPLES, PART 22
Maintaining Your Vision 87

LION'S DEN SURVIVAL PRINCIPLES, PART 23
How to Be Ten Times Better Than the Competition.............. 91

LION'S DEN SURVIVAL PRINCIPLES, PART 24
No Story Is Complete Without an Ending 95

LION'S DEN SURVIVAL PRINCIPLES, CONCLUSION
Getting Beyond Survival 99

LION'S DEN SURVIVAL PRINCIPLES, PART 1
Defining Your Nonnegotiables and Counting the Cost

I remember seeing my friend, the young seminarian, ashen-faced and visibly shaking as he faced the faculty and student body. Each member of our seminary class was required to prepare and deliver a sermon in chapel to the entire school and then to sit through the faculty's public evaluation of the strengths and weaknesses of that effort on the following Friday. Both were terror-filled occasions for the seminarians.

The handsome, baby-faced student shuffled his notes nervously, looked out at the great stone faces of the faculty and blurted out, "I feel like a lion in a den of Daniels."

I've thought often of the insight in that superficially convoluted statement. Is it possible that the often-hostile environment of a media profession can be turned, so that the power resides on the side of the prophets more than on the side of the lions? I think so.

I've wept with a media executive in a major studio who was terminated by her homosexual boss for appearing on Pat Robertson's *700 Club*. I've commiserated with a producer who was relieved of his position for including spiritual content in the series he produced. I've sat through tirades at media trade conventions against "born-againers" and "the religious right" and "Evangelicals" and "fundamentalists" and realized that, at some level, the anger was aimed at *me*. More often, I've felt the pressure of media pros to keep quiet about deep, personal faith because fear of reprisals from peers and bosses was very real and very great.

What are principles for survival in a hostile environment?

Survival Principle: You must have a clear definition of your moral nonnegotiables.

Every person should have a written or mental list of those situations or expectations in which he is willing to risk the job for what's right. When Daniel's king decreed death to all those who prayed to any other God but Him, he crossed Daniel's predetermined "nonnegotiable" line. Daniel had determined that he was willing to risk his job or even his life rather than not pray to Jehovah. The failure to determine what one's personal nonnegotiables are before pressure situations arise invites being pushed into personal, spiritual betrayal when the time of pressure comes.

Survival Principle: You must weigh the immediate cost of defending your righteous standards against the long-term cost of violating them.

The short term, immediate costs of taking a stand are very "now," very real, and very visible. The long-term costs—though often far greater—are very future, very abstract, and nearly invisible.

I watched a Christian director turn down what would have been steady, directorial work on a long-running show because some of the scripts made sport of Jesus Christ. A TV producer was asked to put sex and violence into a series, and he replied, "I'm sure you won't have difficulty finding producers to do that for you, but we don't do sex and violence." Another series producer made it clear that, as a Christian, she wouldn't do material that communicated untrue concepts of God and the supernatural world.

The director was given better work to replace what he lost. The first producer is in high demand because word of his integrity has gotten around. The second producer got the network nod to do the show anyway. In all three cases, in different ways, God took care of them.

Even more important, all three are free from the burden of having sold a piece of their souls for a mere job. They don't have to carry the guilt or discipline of having denied their Master in the interests of Mammon.

Too often, I've heard Christians say, "It's not the kind of work I want to do but . . ." (a) "I need the work," (b) "It'll look good on my resume," or (c) "I hope it will get me to a position where I can do good stuff." Dangerous statements.

You've heard the expression, "His strength is as the strength of ten because his heart is pure." The pure-hearted, graciously unmovable, Christian in media takes on a special kind of power that shuts the mouths of the lions and lionesses in the den. It is God's power, and God's power means omnipotence. Only He is King over the beasts.

LION'S DEN SURVIVAL PRINCIPLES, PART 2
Making a Living vs. Making a Life

"Daniel then said to the guard whom the chief official had appointed over Daniel, Hananiah, Mishael and Azariah, 'Please test your servants for ten days: Give us nothing but vegetables to eat and water to drink. Then, compare our appearance with that of the young men who eat the royal food, and treat your servants in accordance with what you see.' So he agreed to this and tested them for ten days. At the end of the ten days, they looked healthier and better nourished than any of the young men who ate the royal food . . . . At the end of the time set by the king to bring them in, the chief official presented them to Nebuchadnezzar . . . he found none equal to Daniel, Hananiah, Mishael and Azariah . . . ."

— Daniel 1:11-15,18 (NIV)

Pretty stunning, huh? Here we are two and a half millennia after Daniel lived and got tossed to the lions talking about him and the way he dealt with his morally hostile environment. We haven't heard much about the Jewish guys who obeyed the king's order not to pray to any other gods or, for that matter, their kin who did bow down to the image and avoided the fiery furnace. Nonnegotiable virtue has a way of making one memorable in morally hostile environments like Babylon, Hollywood, and other pagan venues!

Survival Principle: Remember that your life is not your career; your life is your character and your quality relationships.

When faced with making "career points" by eating food that violated Jewish law, Daniel made it clear that his moral convictions were more important to him than career success. The one-hundred-people-for-every-job pressure in the entertainment industry and the high financial and personal payoff for "professional success" create constant pressure to believe that "making it in the industry" is everything. It isn't. A prominent executive in a media corporation told me years ago, "I've spent all of my life getting to the top of the ladder, and now I am afraid it's leaning against the wrong wall."

I just learned that the head of a major TV syndication company experienced having his wife take his kids from him and move to the Midwest, because they never saw him anyway. He worked around the clock for so many years making a living that he missed out on living.

Survival Principle: Whether you "make it" or not, life will go on.

Whether you get your break or not, life will go on. Your career can bomb, but character and quality relationships will enable you to live. Your career can soar, but it will not bring fulfillment if you've sold your soul or destroyed your relationships with God and family.

Survival Principle: Never curry favor. Trust God to grant or withdraw it.

The media environment is rife with vain praise, flattery, boot licking, and duplicitous relationships all calculated to procure favor. "Be sincere whether you mean it or not" seems to be a Hollywood approach.

A search of the Scriptures makes it clear that it is God who gives favor; it is God who withdraws it. Being graciously authentic and honest, even when it doesn't seem to be winning friends and influencing people, is always the best approach. Proverbs declares, "When a man's ways are pleasing to the Lord, He makes even his enemies live at peace with Him." (Proverbs 16:7)

Survival Principle: Those who trust the Lord to give favor get ahead farther and faster. Those who curry favor are ultimately despised and ridiculed as weak, untrustworthy, and lacking in integrity.

The success of any work of God is built on this principle. I've watched God give favor with some of America's most powerful media power brokers. I've also watched Him withdraw it on a few occasions. So be it. God will sustain His will, His work, and His way as we trust Him to open doors to people's hearts. Trying to pry them open never ultimately works.

LION'S DEN SURVIVAL PRINCIPLES, PART 3
Watching Out for the Tiny Compromises

". . . Whoever does not fall down and worship will immediately be thrown into a blazing furnace."
— Daniel 3:4-6 (NIV)

Never discount the power of peer pressure. Peer pressure is one of the most powerful forces under heaven. Peer pressure can get you to perform in ways that violate your deepest beliefs and convictions, can get you to do, or not do, things that can cost you deeply in your relationship with God. And few industries are better at harnessing the power of peer pressure to gain conformity than the entertainment industry. In this section, let's consider the "bow-down-or-else" principle.

Not infrequently, it seems that our professional peers in entertainment deliver bow-down-or-face-the-furnace ultimatums. Oh, they're not that direct. It is the suggestion that one who is pro-life is an ideological enemy and not one suitable for a job promotion. It is the inference that one who doesn't cooperate with the "casting couch" practice will never work in the industry. It is the strange looks one gets when one objects to homosexuality as a destructive or morally unacceptable practice. When that pressure is felt, we need survival principles.

Survival Principle: Tend tiny, moral decisions. Your soul is not sold in one great auction; it is bartered away in thousands of tiny trades.

Most moral trades are influenced to some extent by peer pressure. We often make moral "B" choices because they seem, at the time, to be the socially acceptable actions to take. We rationalize these little trades with lines like:

- "I don't want people to think I'm a fanatic/a religious nut/a prude/a Puritan/ narrow minded."
- "I know lots of Christians/ministers/Christian leaders who see nothing wrong with it."
- "Why can't I be a Christian and still be cool/'with it'/on the cutting edge?
- "This isn't a big deal."

Interesting, isn't it, that the officially sanctioned peer pressure, "Bow down and worship or immediately be thrown into a blazing furnace" could have been met with a dynamic equivalent of each of the above arguments. Note, too, that apparently all the rest of the captive Jews did bow down to Nebuchadnezzar's image of gold. They temporarily saved their necks, but they didn't experience the supernatural deliverance and blessing of God.

Years ago I watched a spiritually alive, Christian secretary at a production company sell her soul by degrees to a Jewish atheist boss and end up in heartache. One "B" choice was an all expense paid trip with the man to

England . . . sharing his bedroom. The peer pressure was more than she could handle.

Survival Principle: Seek your security in Christ. Security, for the Christian, is never based on what one can see; it is founded on promises given by a loving, Heavenly Father.

The insecurities of the entertainment industry are nearly overwhelming at times. A prominent actor once told me, "I'm only insecure when I'm working and when I'm not. When I'm working, I'm afraid it won't last, and when I'm not, I'm afraid I'll never get another job."

Those media professionals who have their security in Christ are able to weather the shifting winds of corporate favor, the terrorizing mass layoffs, the horrific political infighting, and the fear of trips to the unemployment line. They know that, as King David said, "I was young and now I am old, yet I have never seen the righteous forsaken or their children begging bread." (Psalm 37:25)

I know a producer who turned down a big project for Steven Spielberg when he had no other work, because it had some occult content that violated his Christian convictions. His unbelieving partner didn't share his beliefs but went along. Since then, this man has been delivered from a number of "fiery furnaces" and has been honored and successful. His security wasn't with Spielberg; it was with the Savior.

This producer didn't overlook a "small" moral decision, and he found his security in Christ. Both good decisions.

LION'S DEN SURVIVAL PRINCIPLES, PART 4
Praying *Before* all Else Has Failed

" . . . Daniel urged his friends to plead for mercy from the God of Heaven concerning this mystery, so that he and his friends might not be executed with the rest of the wise men of Babylon." (v. 18)

— Daniel 2:16-19 (NIV)

I have an idea for a sign I think will sell well in Hollywood. It reads, "Why pray when you can panic?"

In the fast-paced, high-pressure, insecurity-ridden world of professional media, panic seems to push out prayer by an overwhelming factor. In research by Lichter, Lichter, and Rothman into the world of the media elite, it was discovered that the media pros seldom or never pray.

In his hostile environment, Daniel seemed to have the art of "prayer over panic" mastered even as he had other crucial principles of successful living. In fact, he had a well-organized prayer support group!

Survival Principle: Have a godly support group to go to for spiritual support and accountability.

Nebuchadnezzar, in a fit of anger, had just pronounced the death sentence on all of the "magicians, enchanters, sorcerers and astrologers" and "all the wise men of Babylon" because they couldn't tell him (a) what his dream was and (b) the meaning of it. He had decreed that they all be "cut into pieces" and their houses "turned into piles of rubble."

If you were in one of these groups, this could spoil your whole day! This would be worse even than losing your job, not getting the part, missing the big contract, not having your show green-lighted at the network or having the financing on your feature film fall through, now wouldn't it?

After Daniel got more information and had exercised his individual faith by asking the King for time to get the answer, Daniel knew where to go. He went to his godly friends, Hananiah, Mishael, and Azariah AKA Shadrach, Meshach, and Abednego. He'd been with these guys since they were dragged in chains from Jerusalem. They'd gone through the "King's diet crisis" together, the one recorded in chapter one. They would later face the "Bow down or burn" crisis. Daniel, with all his competency and confidence, knew he had to have friends to whom he could go for support.

I am weary of watching bright-eyed, committed young Christian men and women come to Hollywood only to be chewed up and spit out by the Enemy. In fifteen years, you can be sure I have seen more than my share. I also have seen a number who for one or two decades have kept their faith, their convictions, and even their virginity. The difference between these two classes of believers is that the second group has maintained a small support group of spiritual people to whom to go when it's Panic City.

People who enter professional media often are competent, independent, self-starting, confident, and (dare I say it?) arrogant people. This kind of person often thinks he doesn't need anybody else. Wrong, wrong, wrong!

Survival Principle: Mobilize prayer and then listen for the answer.

Daniel "urged [his friends] to plead for mercy from the God of Heaven concerning this mystery." They did so, and then they listened for the answer. It came to Daniel in the middle of the night.

Media professionals are talkers, communicators. They're not known for being great listeners. When you face a panic situation, make your request of the Lord and then shut up and listen until the answer comes—even if you have to listen for what seems to you to be an interminable length of time. P. S. When God does give the answer, spend a generous amount of time praising Him for the answer like Daniel did in verses 19-23!

After all, "Why panic when you can pray . . . and praise?"

LION'S DEN SURVIVAL PRINCIPLES, PART 5
Hanging in There Until Your Big Break Comes

"O King, live forever . . . there is a man in your kingdom who has the spirit of the holy gods in him . . . Call for Daniel and he will tell you what the writing means."

— Daniel 5:10-12 (NIV)

One of the frustrating things about relating to God is that He is not an American! He does not believe in "instant everything." He isn't committed to the "bigger is better" mentality, and time and money don't have any value to Him. He owns all of both. I've observed that God's "un-American" ways rub particularly hard on those in media, especially when vocational work is unfulfilling or nonexistent.

Daniel apparently found a way to handle both being vocationally unfulfilled and unemployed. I want to share some insights on Daniel's incredible ability to cope over the "long haul."

When the frightful finger of God wrote on the wall of Belshazzar's feast, Daniel was unemployed. His influence in the Kingdom had lapsed with the death of Nebuchadnezzar in 562 B.C. This event is 23 years later. When the queen mother punctuated the terror that had gripped the banquet hall with her recommendation, she referred to Daniel's influence clearly in the past tense, "In the time of your father he was found to have insight and intelligence and wisdom like that of the gods." There is no reference to Daniel as a "player" for nearly a quarter of a century.

Many media pros can relate. In an industry filled with wannabes, has-beens, and never-was-gonna-bes there is a more or less constant terror over work. Nagging questions are, "Will I ever work again?" "Am I past my prime?" "Will my break never come?" "Why am I not able to use my God-given talents?" "Is this unchallenging work I must do a sign that I have failed God or that He has abandoned me?"

Daniel seems to have had all these dynamics licked. While we have no direct information, it seems that he must have come to terms with being out of the limelight for so long. He doesn't even make a sarcastic introductory comment like, "Well, now that you're desperate, I get the call. Where have you been for the last two decades?"

Survival Principle: Don't confuse being unfulfilled or out of work with being out of commission. God hasn't forgotten you or abandoned His plans for you.

Daniel was past eighty when the call came from the banquet hall. He had served as vizier or prime minister to the greatest monarch in the world. How soon people forget. He wasn't even invited to this ball held by Nebuchadnezzar's arrogant son! But Daniel wasn't "out of commission." He was obviously still in fellowship with his God, and still had his skills honed for service. He remained "on call."

I know one top media executive who got "dumped" in a corporate shakeup and who turned his unemployment into a blessing by spending quality time with the Lord and his family—things he'd desired for years—rather than sponsoring a "pity party" for himself.

Survival principle: Maintain the kind of character and reputation that will recommend you when the "big job" comes along.

How wonderful that Daniel wasn't passed over to speak for Jehovah to the king because he'd turned bitter toward God for the years of royal disfavor! How terrific that Daniel hadn't disqualified himself for this incredible spiritual task by compromising his spiritual character through immorality, addiction, or vocational work that tarnished his testimony!

I've heard it said, "We'd like to use [fill in the name], but he's become so angry and bitter in the years since his last picture that nobody can work with him." Don't let the "attitude of ingratitude" disqualify you for the big break.

Postscript. According to the Greek historian Herodotus, the very night of the handwriting on the wall the Medo-Persians captured Babylon. Belshazzar was murdered, and Daniel got a fabulous position in the new realm under Darius the Mede, the new king . . . because of his character.

LION'S DEN SURVIVAL PRINCIPLES, PART 6
Establishing the Fact That You Can't Be "Bought"

"Then Daniel answered the king, 'You may keep your gifts for yourself and give your rewards to someone else. Nevertheless, I will read the writing for the king and tell him what it means.'"
— Daniel 5:17 (NIV)

Talk about an opportunity to cash in! Here was the chance of a lifetime. The panicked king Belshazzar, still quaking from the terror of watching a divine hand write mysterious words on the wall of his banquet hall, is willing to give away the company store. He had just made his first offer, "If you can read this writing and tell me what it means, you will be clothed in purple and have a gold chain placed around your neck, and you will be made the third highest ruler in the kingdom."

A typical negotiating response would have been, "How about throwing in an additional robe and a bracelet?" or "Can we talk about the *second* highest slot?" Belshazzar must have been blown away by Daniel's response. In one sentence, Daniel passes on all the prizes behind door "B."

It's clear that Daniel, now an octogenarian, has learned a vital principle of spiritual success.

Survival Principle: Make it clear that, when it comes to doing what's right, you can't be bought.

I watched a Hollywood TV director turn down a series, at least a year's work, because the producers would not commit to avoiding Christ-bashing in their content. I observed a music composer turn down the scoring of a film because it was an exploitation flick. Godly actors turn down parts. A film producer turned down the chance of instant wealth and the status of heading a major division of Spielberg's new company, Dreamworks SKG. A writing team turned down a lucrative project because it glorified the occult. A TV producer passed on a network series unless the content dealing with spiritual things could be changed.

In each case above, the people on the other side were dazzled that (a) any one would turn down lucrative work and (b) that anyone had the kind of moral nonnegotiables that transcended financial gain and personal status. One national survey indicated that 17% of Americans would murder someone if the dollar price were high enough and they were assured of not being caught. Wouldn't you like to know what percentage of Christians in the media would turn down work to obey the Master?

Survival Principle: If your spiritual integrity can be bought at any price, the numbers are meaningless, and Satan will always make sure somebody is in the bidding.

If it can't be bought at any price, it's a waste of his time to try, because you are obviously operating on a different economic system!

Daniel made an additional point with his "pass" on Belshazzar's goodies. He didn't even care if someone else got the stuff offered to him! "Give your rewards to someone else," he said. Some of us find it easier to say "no" to an offer, if it isn't given to somebody else. The true man or woman of God can't be bought, even if the second in line may get the benefit and rub it in.

Survival Principle: What is done with the price offered for our integrity after we turn it down is God's business. In any case, He'll find a way to replace and multiply our reward for faithfulness.

Live by this!

LION'S DEN SURVIVAL PRINCIPLES, PART 7
Dealing with the Power Structure

"Daniel resolved not to defile himself with the royal food and wine, and he asked the chief official for permission not to defile himself in this way. Now God had caused the official to show favor and sympathy to Daniel, but the official told Daniel, 'I am afraid of my Lord the King . . . .'"

— Daniel 1:8-10 (NIV)

Bosses. Everybody has as least one. Every boss has at least one character weakness. Every employee has at least one character weakness. All people have innate tendencies toward rebellion against other people's authority and misuse of their own. Mix these ingredients, and you have the stuff of which power struggles, bitter conflict, and lawsuits are made. The world of media has its share of unreasonable, egomaniacal, unethical, and exploitive bosses. The narcissistic producer and screaming director are legendary Hollywood stereotypes. A feature film built around one such producer was titled, *The S. O. B.*

Daniel worked for some of the worst bosses in human history. Tyrannical King Nebuchadnezzar, Saddam

Hussein's cultural ancestor, dragged him to Babylon in the first place in a ruthless ploy. Daniel was pulled out of retirement and worked just one night for Belshazzar, a despot so arrogant and evil he took confiscated sacred vessels from the temple of Jehovah and used them for party dishes. Later, Daniel worked for Darius the Mede who was such an egomaniac that he signed a decree that anyone not praying exclusively to him should be fed to lions. And you thought your boss was bad!

Survival Principle: Bosses are to be respected but not feared, because they have no ultimate authority.

Daniel's immediate supervisor was terrorized by his boss, King Nebuchadnezzar. Daniel was afraid of neither. Daniel knew that no human boss makes ultimate decisions. Proverb 21:1 declares, "The king's heart is in the hand of the Lord; He directs it like water in an irrigation ditch." When a person is resting in the care of his Heavenly Father, God defies hell itself to mess with His plans for His child! Certainly no mere boss can.

Survival Principle: In matters of conscience, we must prayerfully prepare an open appeal to the authority, one that supports his objectives.

In the conscience matter of food forbidden by His God, Daniel rejected misguided—but commonly used—approaches like the following:

- He didn't rebel against the authority and refuse to submit ("You can't make me eat this non-Kosher garbage!").

- He didn't undermine the authority by pretending to eat it when the boss was looking and sneak in his own food when he wasn't.
- He didn't speak evil of his "godless" and "pagan" supervisor and thereby spread rebellion and slander his name.

Having "resolved not to defile himself," he dealt with the matter openly, trusting God to give him favor.

Survival Principle: When faced with directives that violate your conscience, provide a creative solution that will enhance your boss's image and success . . . and protect your own integrity.

Having been in management all of my life, I've come to resist workers who dump problems on my desk, but make no efforts on their own to propose creative solutions for them. Equally offensive are workers who seek solutions that make everybody else's job more difficult but their own. As you recall, Daniel proposed a ten-day "food experiment" and was willing to take the consequences if the plan failed. Because God favored the plan, Daniel got the decision he wanted, and the boss ended up looking even better in the "royal review of servants!"

Note: None of these principles is conditioned on your boss's being a nice, reasonable, or righteous person. In fact, your character is more greatly enhanced in dealing righteously with an impossible boss than in dealing with a saintly one. And the dramatic enhancement of the character of Christ in you is the name of God's game!

LION'S DEN SURVIVAL PRINCIPLES, PART 8
How to Frustrate Your Enemies

"At this, the administrators and satraps tried to find grounds for charges against Daniel in his conduct of government affairs, but they were unable to do so. They could find no corruption in him, because he was trustworthy and neither corrupt nor negligent. Finally, these men said, 'We will never find any basis for charges against this man Daniel unless it has something to do with the Law of his God.'"

— Daniel 6:4-5 (NIV)

When I was a kid, I was a bellhop in a Christian resort hotel. One of the fascinating characters who came to the hotel each summer was a chess Grandmaster. Because of his reputation, chess players from miles around would come to challenge him. I remember his playing twelve players at a time on boards lined up in a row on tables in the large lobby of the hotel. He had such a photographic memory he would know on all twelve boards if an opponent made an improper move!

This man befriended me and would explain chess strategy to me, a very amateur player. One thing stuck with me. He said, "Larry, people who don't know chess don't place much value on the pawn. They will sacrifice one with little concern. That's foolhardy. You give me a one pawn advantage and I will whip any chess player in the world." Great chess players, like great military strategists, know the value of not giving the opponent any advantage, of not "giving ground."

Daniel knew this same principle. He lived his life in such a way that he did not "give ground" to his adversaries in any area of his life. The verses quoted at the head of this section are stunners to me. By the admission of Daniel's own enemies, preoccupation with matters of his faith was Daniel's only aberration. His life, work and character were impeccable.

Survival Principle: Tend well every area of your life and work. Not to do so gives your enemies an advantage.

Play loose with your work responsibilities, and someone else will exploit this negligence to get your job. Abandon the needs of your spouse and family, and the erosion in your home will wash away the foundation of your life and work. Buy into the "little white lie" approach to total truthfulness and transparency, and watch the Enemy undermine your personal and professional credibility.

Survival Principle: Be willing to be viewed as a fanatic to pursue your relationship with God and practice your faith.

Someone once said, "If someone won't miss a ball game, they're a 'fan.' If they won't miss Bible study, they're a 'fanatic.'" Extremism in the pursuit of God is no sin; mediocrity is no virtue. An agent's assistant told me of being asked by coworkers where she was going as she left the office. To her associates' surprise, she declared without embarrassment, "I'm going to my Bible study." On a visit to Warner Brothers studios, I noticed a small picture of Jesus tacked to the wall of a secretarial bay along side pictures of the secretary's children. I said to her, "Are you a follower of that man?" Without a moment's hesitation she said, "He's my best friend."

The truly faithful are commonly accused of "fanaticism" by the unfaithful. Deal with it.

Could our enemies say of us that they could find no fault, no "corruption," and no "negligence"? If so, this is proof that we have not "given ground" to them. Ephesians 4:27 declares, "Do not give the Devil a foothold." Daniel didn't, and it worked for him.

LION'S DEN SURVIVAL PRINCIPLES, PART 9
Obedience Over Consequence

"O Nebuchadnezzar, we do not need to defend ourselves before you in this matter. If we are thrown into the blazing furnace, the God we serve is able to save us from it, and he will rescue us from you hand, O King. But, even if he does not, we want you to know, O King, that we will not serve your gods or worship the image of gold you have set up."
— Daniel 3:16-18 (NIV)

"It's your show, and you can do what you want with it, but we do not do five minute rape scenes." With this line, the Christian writer-producer made a moral principle clear to one of the most powerful men in Hollywood. He knew full well the statement could cost him his working relationship with the mogul and separate him from the network television series on which they were collaborating. This and other moral issues eventually did result in a separation of ways, but you can be sure of one thing. The word got around that there was someone in Hollywood who answered to a Higher Authority.

Spiritual authority is something that most media power brokers do not understand. They understand positional authority, financial power, and intimidation, but not spiritual authority. To survive as a Christian in the often-hostile environment of media, one must possess it. Spiritual authority is the power a believer derives from being identified so completely with Christ that His power neutralizes all threats, fears, and forces.

That the three valiant Jewish men in Daniel 3 possessed spiritual power is clear from their response to the life-threatening situation they faced. The first proof is that they felt no need to argue or defend themselves.

Survival Principle: *Those with spiritual authority in their lives never have to argue or defend themselves.*

"We do not need to defend ourselves before you in this matter" was their statement of divine confidence. In his powerful book, *Spiritual Authority*, Watchman Nee says, "God doesn't argue," and the one who possesses His power doesn't either. Only those insecure in their power or position get defensive or argumentative.

The second proof that Shadrach, Meshach and Abednego were tapped into God's power was that they were totally unshakable.

Survival Principle: *Those whose lives are built on the foundation of their faith in an all-powerful God are unshakable.*

The Christian who trembles in fear of man's consequences and violates God's law to accommodate human threats doesn't understand God's power or His consequences. "The God we serve is able to save us . . .

and he will rescue us from your hand . . ." was the way the Israelite men expressed their confidence in the power they possessed in God's care. I'm convinced that the only ones able to deal successfully with the insecurities, pressures, threats, intimidations, and occult principalities at work in media are believers who are secure in God's defense of them.

The three Hebrew slaves then made a stunning declaration which indicated they had not lost touch with unpleasant reality. They boldly declared, "But even if he does not [save us], we want you to know, O King, that we will not serve your gods or worship the image of gold you have set up." In saying this, the three acknowledged they did not possess the full knowledge of God's plan for their lives . . . and that, sometimes, things don't turn out well for God's followers. But, they could see beyond present circumstances to distant benefits.

Survival Principle: *Count on the long-term rewards of obedience, even if the short-term situation goes against you.*

The writer-producer above had three other professional opportunities in hand within one hour after being let go for not supporting the values of the executive producer of the show.

LION'S DEN SURVIVAL PRINCIPLES, PART 10
A Spirit That Sets You Apart

King Nebuchadnezzar: "When the magicians, enchanters, astrologers, and diviners came, I told them the dream, but they could not interpret it for me. Finally, Daniel came into my presence, and . . . I said, I know that the spirit of the holy gods is in you, and no mystery is too difficult for you."
— Daniel 4:7-9 (NIV)

A veteran TV director was directing a series for a producer known not to be a Christian. After working with the director for a while, the producer said to him, "You don't swear, do you?" "No, I don't." Nothing more was said until sometime later when the producer observed, "You seem to be the kind of person who has had a life-changing experience. Is that the case?" "Yes, that is exactly the case." "Do you mind my asking what it was?" "It was Jesus Christ." After a moment to digest the answer, the producer said, "Maybe that's what I need." The director responded, "He's exactly what you need. I guarantee it." The director's spirit drew the questions.

All human beings have a mark of individuality more precise than either their fingerprints or their DNA patterns. It's their spirit. While most people don't become adept at "reading spirits," they walk away from others with a subconscious realization of the kind and character of the spirit others possess. They know they have been in the presence of a bitter spirit, an angry spirit, a joyful spirit, a lighthearted spirit, a lustful spirit, a greedy spirit, a proud spirit, a threatening spirit, a humble spirit, a serving spirit, a wise spirit, or a spirit with some other attribute. The spirit of a person communicates non-verbally even more powerfully than verbally! One "senses" another's spirit even when not consciously thinking about it.

Daniel had distinguished himself by his spirit to such an extent that when the king called Daniel into his presence, he commented on this unique attribute of the man. "I know that the spirit of the holy gods is in you" was the way he put it. That was a fine compliment for a devout believer.

Survival Principle: Allow your human spirit or personality to be totally possessed and dominated by the Spirit of Christ.

John the Baptist described this phenomenon as, "He must become greater; I must become less." (John 3:30)

Believers who take on the spirit of those unbelievers around them become spiritually invisible, an indistinguishable part of the pagan herd. They lose all personal magnetism and divine attractiveness. Those who are filled and controlled by "the spirit of the holy" (the Holy Spirit of Christ) are instantly and continually (a) attractive to seekers and (b) repulsive to the wicked. Either way, the person is unforgettable!

On a previous shoot, an executive producer had watched as the same Spirit-filled director mentioned above handled one crisis after another with a tranquil spirit. She remarked, "I don't know what you're on, but I want some of it." He replied, "I'm on a mega-dose of the Holy Spirit." And, indeed, he was. It showed.

LION'S DEN SURVIVAL PRINCIPLES, PART 11
Giving Credit Where Credit Is Due

"The king asked Daniel . . . 'Are you able to tell me what I saw in my dream and interpret it?' Daniel replied, 'No wise man, enchanter, magician or diviner can explain to the king the mystery he has asked about, but there is a God in heaven who reveals mysteries. He has shown King Nebuchadnezzar what will happen in days to come.'"

— Daniel 2:26-27 (NIV)

In an industry where verbal and legal "credit wars" are waged over whose name is listed first, whose name has bigger letters, and what title is given, it's no mystery that God seldom gets top billing. He's in competition with too many competing "gods."

If the media is nothing else, it is a place where the human ego is given extremely clear and visible expression. One executive told me at a major media convention that studio executives would berate the limousine company and demand a different vehicle if they discovered that another exec had a longer limo than theirs—one of many measures of rank and status.

If the king had asked many media executives if they could disclose and interpret his dream, the responses may have ranged from "Of course, I can; don't you know who I am?" to "Do it yourself. Can't you see I'm busy?" Daniel's response was quite different. He had learned a powerful lesson.

Survival Principle: Give God credit for all the good He does. To cop part of the credit is to ask to be humbled.

Since God doesn't share His glory with anybody, those who steal part of it are entering a fight they cannot win—a war of the "gods." They will end up crushed.

Not only did Daniel not boast about what he might (wrongfully) have called his own powers to know and interpret mysteries, he made it clear that what the true and living God does can't be duplicated even by occult powers. "No wise man, enchanter, magician, or diviner" can do such things. He made it unmistakably clear that it was the work of "God in heaven."

In contrasting God with the other spirits and their devotees, Daniel enhanced the majesty of Jehovah, plus, he let no praise for himself come from his own lips. In so doing, Daniel qualified for exaltation by the God whose glory he never coveted. Matthew 23:12 declares that God exalts those who humble themselves.

And exalted he was!

LION'S DEN SURVIVAL PRINCIPLES, PART 12
How to Weather Adversity

"Now when Daniel learned that the decree had been published, he went home to his upstairs room where the windows opened toward Jerusalem. Three times a day he got down on his knees and prayed giving thanks to his God, just as he had done before. Then these men went as a group and found Daniel praying and asking God for help."

— Daniel 6:10-11 (NIV)

The "sixtyish" woman was standing in the hall of the executive suite of one of the big three networks. Surrounded by boxes, she was leaning against the wall weeping. "Ruth," I said, "What's wrong?" "After I've worked my heart out for 27 years for this network they gave me three days notice." She had been summarily "outplaced."

Certainly, nobody goes into a media profession for security. Situations can turn quickly. A corporate takeover dumps all the "other company's" people in the drink. Mercurial company politics suddenly leave a faithful employee "odd man out." Even the discovery of a devout,

Christian faith can result in a competent employee's suddenly being excluded from the leadership circle.

Daniel got ripped off in a political scheme. His enemies, knowing Daniel's only point of vulnerability was in matters of his faith (Daniel 6:5), played on the king's pride and snookered him into decreeing the death penalty to anyone who prayed to someone other than the king himself.

To Daniel, this was more than the imminent possibility of losing his job. It was the legal guarantee of losing his life! Daniel's response provides a dynamite survival principle when we face adversity:

Survival Principle: When all hell breaks loose, keep praying prayers of thanksgiving.

Back in his room, Daniel continued "giving thanks to his God just as he had done before." Giving thanks in adversity, not necessarily for adversity, is a primary hallmark of the person of faith. Giving thanks in the middle of an unresolved catastrophe (1) proves we trust Somebody Bigger than the crisis, (2) proves our mind, heart, and soul are not tied to the phony "securities" (or threats) of the temporal world, and (3) shows we aren't willing to insult our King by forgetting all the other messes He has pulled us through in the past. A continuing "attitude of gratitude" in our prayers keeps us focused above the fray and on the Father.

When catastrophe strikes, get on your knees and give thanks. Then, keep giving thanks until things get better. Or don't—it's your peace and faith you're risking.

LION'S DEN SURVIVAL PRINCIPLES, PART 13
Surviving the Fire

"Then King Nebuchadnezzar leaped to his feet in amazement and asked his advisers, 'Weren't there three men that we tied up and threw into the fire?' They replied, 'Certainly, O king.' He said, 'Look! I see four men walking around in the fire, unbound and unharmed, and the fourth looks like a son of the gods.'"

— Daniel 3:24-25 (NIV)

"Into every life a little rain must fall" is only part of the story. Most believers have discovered that going through fire is just as common as going through rain. Rain is merely a temporary unpleasantness that does a lot of good overall. Fire is a destructive, all-consuming threat to our very existence. We experience fires of adversity, fires of interpersonal conflict, fires of rejection and heartache, fires of financial need, fires of injustice and exploitation, and fires of physical illness and disease. Experiencing fire is no fun!

God knows we will go through the fires of testing in various ways, so He illustrates methods of handling these testings through the story of Shadrach, Meshach, and Abednego.

Survival Principle: When you're going through the fire, you don't have to be in bondage to it.

Daniel 3:25 says that the three Hebrew men in the fire were "walking around unbound . . . ." They had been bound when they were thrown into the fire, but now they were free. Often, it is actually the fire of testing that frees us from bondage to besetting sins, addictions, and destructive patterns of thought and attitude.

How many an addict has refused to change until he ended up in prison? How many an angry man has refused to deal with his ill-managed anger until it cost him his marriage? How many an immoral young girl has persisted in her impure lifestyle until she got an unwanted pregnancy? It is often the suffering of fiery experiences that breaks the bonds of sin in our lives . . . if we let it.

Bible teacher Tim Storey advises, "When you go through hell, don't stay there!" When you go through the fire, don't let it conquer you. In the power of Christ, conquer it, and let it free you.

Survival Principle: Whether you can see Him or not, the Son of God is never closer to you than in your adversity. Count on it!

Does a righteous father not rush to the aid of his child when he is in danger? Can a loving mother stay away from the bedside of her injured child? Does not a loving friend hold you more tightly and defend you more strongly when you are being attacked? The Bible's declaration that Christ "never leaves us nor forsakes us" is certainly even more true when we are in the midst of adversity. Count on His presence and draw on His strength to quench the flames.

Survival Principle: Respond in such a way in adversity that others can see the Son of God in you, whether you are consciously aware of His presence or not.

By reading Daniel's account, we have no evidence that Shadrach, Meshach, and Abednego could see the "fourth man" in the fire with them! There's no record of their touching him, talking with him, or being aware of him at all. When they stepped out of the furnace, he was nowhere to be found or seen. Onlookers, however, could clearly see the image of one "like a son of the gods" in the furnace. If we surrender to the filling of the Spirit in the midst of our adversity, others will see Him. If we don't, they'll see us . . . at our worst!

LION'S DEN SURVIVAL PRINCIPLES, PART 14
How to Get Demoted

"Is this not the great Babylon I have built as the royal residence, by my mighty power and for the glory of my majesty?"
— Daniel 4:28-30 (NIV)

"In one sense," said the earnest Christian TV director, "I have to promote myself every day. As a freelance professional, if I don't promote myself, who will?" In so saying, he put the finger on one of the tough balancing acts Christians in media face on a daily basis . . . where does successful, professional salesmanship and promotion end and sinful, pride-driven self-exaltation begin?

One thing is sure. God doesn't share His glory with anybody. He is a "jealous" God according the Scriptures. This means that—knowing He deserves all glory—He becomes the antagonist of anyone who seeks to steal some of it. Lucifer learned this the hard way when he was tired of being Number Two to God (Isaiah 14:12-15). He was cast out of heaven and doomed to perdition. The same hard lesson reduced King Nebuchadnezzar to animal behavior for the statement cited above. He ended up suffering seven years of debilitating, mental illness for his arrogant claim to credit that was rightfully his Maker's.

Survival Principle: God doesn't mind our displaying the talents, skills, and successes in our lives so long as we make it unmistakably clear that He is the source of them all.

Nebuchadnezzar was the recipient of incredible, divine favor and blessing upon himself and his kingdom and claimed credit for it all personally. Daniel, on the other hand, was offered rich rewards for interpreting the handwriting on the wall in Daniel 5:17, but he asked that they be given to someone else. He knew his awesome ability to interpret dreams and visions was totally God's work in and through him. Nebuchadnezzar was demoted and Daniel was promoted!

Survival Principle: There are few limits to how much success we can enjoy, if we don't care who gets the credit for it.

Daniel knew that his personal and professional destiny was not correlated directly with the extent of successful, self-promotion he could generate on his own behalf. He had no agent, no publicist, and no team of media spin-doctors. He wasted no time trying to convince others how terrific and competent he was. He had a deep and unshakable faith in the true and living God and knew that his promotion would be directly linked to his faithful service to and exaltation of his Master. Sure enough, that turned out to be the key to his success.

Survival Principle: Exalt yourself and God will demote you. Humble yourself before Him, and He will lift you up.

Jesus himself proclaimed this principle!

Another freelance professional in Hollywood fired his agent as he began to trust more and more in his Savior. He wrote his own version of Psalm 23:1, "The Lord is my agent. I shall not want." He notes that he's had much more steady work since he made that decision. It figures.

LION'S DEN SURVIVAL PRINCIPLES, PART 15
Identifying With the Sins of Your Community

" . . . O, Lord, the great and awesome God . . .we have sinned and done wrong. We have been wicked and rebelled; we have turned away from your commands and laws. We have not listened to your servants the prophets, who spoke in your name to our kings, our princes, and our fathers, and to all the people of the land. All Israel has transgressed your law and turned away, refusing to obey you."

— Daniel 9:4-6 (NIV)

The woman manager at one of the big three networks expressed her grief at the moral impurity of her employer's programming. "Sometimes I feel dirty taking a paycheck from a company that would air such hideous stuff," she said. She asked for prayer as to whether she should stay in her job, even though she was in the financial controls department far removed from network program decisions.

"Wait a minute!" you say. "She can't accept responsibility for what other people do! It's not her fault if those in her company make decisions or produce product which pollutes the moral environment, steals the innocence of children, or defies the laws of God."

In Daniel's awesome prayer for his people in Daniel 9:4-19, he clearly identifies himself with behaviors in which he, personally, had no part. He catalogs the sins of his community in extremely graphic terms—wickedness, rebellion, turning from God's laws, refusing to listen to the prophets, and such. The attributes he describes could not have been further from his personal pattern of life and godliness. Yet, here he is, accepting some level of responsibility—of social and moral concern. He intercedes on behalf of his own sinful people and pleads with God for forgiveness and mercy. He says, "We do not make requests of you because we are righteous, but because of your great mercy." (Daniel 9:18)

Survival principle: Believers in a hostile environment cannot "hole up" in some underground bunker as the war rages overhead. They must take up arms with the weapons of the Spirit and intercede on behalf of the collective war effort and even the sins of others.

I've thought of placing signs around Hollywood that say, "Is all of Hollywood going to hell . . . or it is just me?" In this insanely individualistic American society, we Christians sometimes think the sin around us is far removed from our personal lives and responsibilities.

Wrong. Godly people recognize that they are "priests," "mediators," and "agents of redemption" of the pagan society around them. They know they are providentially placed in the midst of evildoers and evil works to do what they can to redeem the lost people and the evil practices.

If all of Hollywood goes to hell, the believers in Hollywood will both suffer serious consequences and bear some collective, spiritual responsibility. The same holds true for the setting in which you serve.

Get involved. What if God is withholding his redemption of your company, studio, network, or profession until you intercede with Him on its behalf?

LION'S DEN SURVIVAL PRINCIPLES, PART 16
Discovering the Power of Praise Over Problems

"Then Daniel praised the God of heaven and said, 'Praise be to the name of God for ever and ever; wisdom and power are his. He changes times and seasons; he sets up kings and deposes them. He gives wisdom to the wise and knowledge to the discerning. He reveals deep and hidden things; he knows what lies in darkness and light dwells with him.'"
— Daniel 2:19b-22 (NIV)

As a person who has been accused of being "terminally positive," I'm not given to fits of rage, depression, or hopelessness. Consequently, creeping coldness in my relationship with Jesus Christ is recognizable not by the presence of the negative so much as by the absence of the positive. I simply lose my attitude of praise.

A spirit of praise that was independent of circumstances marked Daniel—like all mightily used servants of God. This praise passage, only partially quoted above, was uttered when Daniel, his friends, and all the other spiritual advisors in the land were on death row! Nebuchadnezzar had made an absolutely impossible and unreasonable demand of all this spiritual advisors—not only to interpret a dream, but to describe the dream in detail before interpreting it! When the phony advisors fudged, he ordered them all slaughtered.

The other advisors panicked, cried "Foul!" and desperately sought to manipulate the king to change his decision. Not Daniel. He mobilized prayer and, in faith, asked for time to allow His God to work.

Survival Principle: When all hell breaks loose, don't fight it; call on heaven to handle it. In the long run, heaven can always handle hell!

At the darkest hour in the lives of his compatriots, Daniel was composing a praise song (it's written in poetry!). Sure, God had just given him a revelation of the mystery, but Daniel had yet to present the information to the King, and the sword still hung over his head. Nebuchadnezzar was hardly a man who backed down from his demands, even when they were met! Nonetheless, Daniel praised his God.

Survival Principle: In a crisis, one word from the Lord is better than ten thousand from anyone else.

So he praised. Did he ever praise! He praised God's name, His wisdom, His power, and His sovereignty, His generous sharing of His insights, His omniscience, and His light-filled character. Daniel knew that the circumstances were such that he couldn't control them, so he might as well glorify the One who could.

Survival Principle: Praise is the agent that stills the tempest in the hearts of believers when God chooses not to still the tempest around them.

Going through hell? Call on heaven, listen for a word from God, and generate a song of praise. It surely beats the alternative.

LION'S DEN SURVIVAL PRINCIPLES, PART 17
Waiting until the "Last Chapter" is Written

"Then King Darius wrote to all the peoples, nations and men of every language throughout the land: ' . . . I issue a decree that . . . people must fear and reverence the God of Daniel. For he is the living God, and he endures forever . . . . He has rescued Daniel from the power of the lions.' So Daniel prospered during the reign of Darius and the reign of Cyrus the Persian."
— Daniel 6:26-28 (NIV)

You've seen it happen. The home team is down three touchdowns in the last quarter of play. The stands begin to empty, so that by the time the clock shows 05:00 minutes left, there are empty seats everywhere. Then, through some miracle of resurrected motivation or unexpected events, the home team comes back! With 00:14 showing on the clock, it scores the winning touchdown, and joyful pandemonium prevails!

The curses of those fans—halfway home in their cars and listening on their radios—are audible throughout the city. If only they had stayed until the end!

Daniel always stayed around to the end, until his God had written the last chapter, until victory emerged. He kept on believing until deliverance came. He did have one advantage. He wasn't an American—an impatient, time-obsessed, instant-everything, quick-fix American. It was culturally more acceptable for him to persevere . . . until the final victory.

Too many believers fail to appreciate that profound Yogi Berraism, "It ain't over 'til it's over." Things look bleak. The opposition is overwhelming. Resources are depleted. Energy to keep fighting is gone. Circumstances are all adverse. So, they give up—lose heart—in what they perceive to be "sure defeat." They throw in the towel before the fight is really over. Then, stunningly, victory emerges from the jaws of defeat. Their God reveals Himself in power!

Survival Principle: Hang in there until God finishes His work. Leaving one second before God brings victory is catastrophic; hanging around ten years after He does is sharing in the spoils.

Suppose, after 40 years herding sheep, Moses had taken his life in despair the day before the burning bush. Suppose Judas had waited just 14 more days before deciding to betray Jesus, leaving the Romans' with Jesus' blood on their hands and himself a dazzled follower of the risen Christ. Suppose Daniel had slashed his wrists in panic upon being tossed into the den of lions.

Survival Principle: Difficulty is not a reliable indicator of impending defeat, because it is also the typical setting in which victory is secured.

Survival Principle: Difficulty is the environment for miracle, unless it is to be a very great miracle; then, the environment is impossibility.

Upon Daniel's emergence from the den, the following happened: Darius issued an international decree that every subject must worship Daniel's God (!), he composed a poetic tribute to Jehovah for all the people to hear, and he set Daniel up so securely that he "prospered" during the reign of Darius and his successor! All this occurred because Daniel was willing to wait for God. To wait for God is to wait for Good.

LION'S DEN SURVIVAL PRINCIPLES, PART 18
Getting Past Ego to Reach Understanding

"Do not be afraid, Daniel. Since the first day that you set your mind to gain understanding and to humble yourself before your God, your words were heard, and I have come in response to them."

— Daniel 10:12 (NIV)

Has it ever seemed to you that the entertainment business, especially film and television, has more than its share of people with enormous egos? In your mind, run through the instantly recognizable names in power in media, and it will be difficult to name one known for humility. My father had a tongue-in-cheek observation about a "big ego" person: "I'd like to buy him for what he's worth and sell him for what he thinks he's worth." It's frightening how much ego devalues us by getting in the way of both understanding and spiritual usability.

When God's messenger speaks to Daniel in the above passage, he associates Daniel's divine favor with two personal starting points: the point at which Daniel "set his mind to gain understanding" and the point at he "humbled himself before his God."

Survival Principle: Gain understanding; it is far more valuable than wealth, power, or prestige.

A person filled with himself or herself is not interested in gaining understanding, only in being heard and in being recognized. Proverbs says it this way: "A fool finds no pleasure in understanding but delights in airing his own opinions." (Daniel 18:2) Favor with God and others begins with seeking not to be understood, but to understand.

Survival Principle: You learn nothing with your tongue loose; that's why it's one of the few organs God made with its own cage.

The second starting point for Daniel's success was the day he set out to "humble himself before his God." In our society in general, and in media in particular, there is little market for humble people, especially those who humble themselves before God. Yet, this is why Daniel is addressed by God's messenger a few verses earlier, "you who are highly esteemed." Daniel joyfully accepted his position in the Cosmic Pecking Order. This took him out of competition with God and put him in concert with Him. God, then, "heard his words and came to him."

Survival Principle: God ultimately doesn't bless the self-made man; he'll just worship his maker more fervently.

Seek understanding and humble yourself before God. He'll listen to you and come to you, too!

LION'S DEN SURVIVAL PRINCIPLES, PART 19
How to Acquire Good References

" . . . If a country sins against me by being unfaithful and I stretch out my hand against it . . . even if these three men—Noah, Daniel, and Job—were in it, they could save only themselves by their righteousness, declares the Sovereign Lord."
— Ezekiel 14:12-14 (NIV)

A Hollywood actor once said a performer goes through stages in his career that are reflected by what producers say about him. The progression is: (1) "Who's Joe Doaks?" (2) "We can't afford a star, why don't we use Joe Doaks?" (3) "It would really make this picture if we could just get Joe Doaks." (4) "What we need is a young Joe Doaks." (5) "Who's Joe Doaks?" The perceptions shift despite little or no change in the person's talent.

Unfortunately, what other people think and say is much too important to most media professionals. While "a good name is more desirable than great wealth" (Proverbs 22:1), there is only one character reference that really counts. It is not what our peers say about us. It is what God says about us.

In the Ezekiel passage quoted above, God Himself holds Daniel up with Noah and Job as examples of extraordinary virtue. He states that His anger is so inflamed at Israel because of its moral apostasy that even if all three of these heroes of the faith were in national prominence, their stellar righteousness could spare only themselves from His judgment and no one else.

In addition to the character reference of "The Sovereign Lord" above, Jesus also certifies Daniel's credibility by affirming one his prophetic visions in Matthew 24:15. Not bad character references!

Survival Principle: If you want God to speak well of you in times to come, you have to pursue His will and way today.

Daniel pursued a lifelong quest to worship and obey his God—come hell or high water, royal edict or fiery furnace, palace conspiracy or lion's den. He had little concern for what people thought of him; He wanted God to think well of him . . . and God did.

It's amazing how a single-minded pursuit of pleasing God brings the flaky and often ill-motivated opinions of others into immediate perspective. In the grand scheme of things, they don't count for much.

In fact, Jesus noted that being well spoken of by others should be a matter of concern: "Woe to you when all men speak well of you, for that is how their fathers treated the false prophets." (Luke 6:26)

Survival Principle: Don't be preoccupied with status. Pursue stature, and status—with God and man—will be your reward.

LION'S DEN SURVIVAL PRINCIPLES, PART 20
How to Pray And Be Heard

**"Now, our God, hear the prayers and petitions of your servant
. . . we do not make requests of you because we are righteous,
but because of your great mercy."**
— Daniel 9:17-18 (NIV)

Parenting six children into adulthood is a formidable task. One of the challenges is helping each child understand how to make requests that are likely to be heard and answered. In our home, we used the concept of "magic words"—words like "please" and "thank you." My wife and I tended not to respond to requests that were expressed as demands, ones spoken in arrogance, or ones that lacked the appropriate "magic words." How many times we prompted, "Can you say the magic word?" Commonly, the question was met with a more contrite, "Please?" I also remember, more than once, correcting a child when he asked something of my wife disrespectfully, "Remember to whom you're speaking!"

Daniel knew God's "magic words" in prayer, the words to which He surely responds. Daniel shows this in his awesome petition for Israel in Daniel 9:4-19. This prayer of nearly 500 words is filled with magic words like "We have sinned," "We have been wicked," and "We have rebelled." Daniel makes reference to his nation's sin and moral depravity more than twenty times in a prayer that would be fewer than two typewritten pages!

Survival Principle: *If you want God to hear your prayers, be sure you acknowledge and express that you don't deserve to be heard.*

Jesus made this same point as He defined the kind of prayers God hears in Luke 18:10-14. The Pharisee was not heard because his prayer made it clear that he thought he deserved to be heard. The tax collector was heard with his prayer (delivered while beating his breast), "God have mercy on me a sinner." It was transparently undeserving.

Daniel was lavish in his expressions of repentance and contrition, because he knew to whom he was speaking— the perfect, holy, sinless, completely righteous God of Heaven who can tolerate not even one hint of sin.

Survival Principle: *In prayer, remember to whom you are speaking, or God won't "remember" what you say.*

When I complained to a local policeman at a Rotary Club luncheon that I thought it was a waste of police resources to cite speeders on the street behind my house when there were more terrible crimes being committed in our city, he said tersely, "Nobody gets as many tickets as he deserves." Daniel, remembering that "with God nobody gets what he truly deserves," made his prayers on the basis of God's mercy, not his own merit.

Survival Principle: Never ask God for what you deserve; that's asking for hell. You don't want justice! Beg for mercy.

LION'S DEN SURVIVAL PRINCIPLES, PART 21
Letting God Have Your Enemies for Lunch

"And when Daniel was lifted from the den, no wound was found on him, because he had trusted in his God. At the king's command, the men who had falsely accused Daniel were brought in and thrown into the lion's den, along with their wives and children. And before they reached the floor of the den, the lions overpowered them and crushed all their bones."
— Daniel 6:23b-24 (NIV)

In the Southern California culture where people communicate as much by bumper sticker as by the spoken word, "I DON'T GET MAD. I GET EVEN" is a common message. The creator of the concept, I presume, has had one miserable life, because living by vengeance rather than by forgiveness violates a key principle for successful living.

We all read—and love—the part of Daniel's story in which he experiences deliverance from the supernaturally-closed mouths of the lions. Seldom do we read—and relish—the part about the supernaturally-opened mouths for Daniel's enemies. And yet the message is that God takes care of His kids. Implicit in the passage is a key survival principle: God desires a monopoly in the justice business, so he never delegates personal revenge to his followers.

Curiously absent from the story of Daniel's victimization by a steady string of enemies is any indication that he (a) hated them, (b) defended himself against them, or (c) sought revenge. In fact, when the explanation for his deliverance from the lions is given in the above passage, it is singular: "No wound was found on him, because he trusted in His God."

Survival Principle: Allowing exploitation to drive us deeper into trust is far superior to allowing it to drive us into bitterness.

The reason for this is simple. God will traverse land and sea, heaven and hell to defend—and avenge—the one who trusts implicitly and fully in Him.

Survival Principle: God's defense of His faithful ones is far more effective and comprehensive than our feeble attempts to defend ourselves.

If Daniel had sought to defend himself, he would have been the grand loser. The vengeful motivation would have stolen the joy of his relationship with God. His self-orchestrated solution would have been mundane human stuff—not miracle stuff. And—the judgment would not have been so comprehensive. God even dealt with his enemies' family members. He had the whole bunch for lunch!

How about bumper stickers that say, "I DON'T GET MAD. I GET *SPIRITUAL*."? The result would be far better!

LION'S DEN SURVIVAL PRINCIPLES, PART 22
Maintaining Your Vision

" . . . The God of heaven will set up a kingdom that will never be destroyed, nor will it be left to another people. It will crush all those kingdoms and bring them to an end, but it will itself endure forever. This is the meaning of the vision of the rock cut out of a mountain, but not by human hands—a rock that broke the iron, the bronze, the clay, the silver and the gold to pieces."

— Daniel 2:44 (NIV)

One of the first things that is lost in difficult times and hostile circumstances is our vision of ultimate victory. No matter how many times we read the promises of God's Book, no matter how familiar the "glory songs" of the Christian faith are to us, they all tend to vanish like breath in adversity.

Daniel knew hard times. It was no fun having the hated Babylonians sweep into his homeland, demolish his city, slaughter the warriors, rape his female kin, steal the plunder, poke out the eyes out his king, and drag Daniel and his compatriots off as slaves. It was no fun for a faithful Jewish youth to be forced to eat non-Kosher food and learn the language and pagan ways of idolaters. It was no fun having to give up his name, Daniel, which meant "God is my Judge" for Belteshazzar, which glorified the pagan god Bel!

Through the king's dream, Daniel received a "victory vision" of the future that not only drove Nebuchadnezzar to his knees (2:46), but also provided perspective to Daniel for the rest of His life. It was the vision of an unshakable kingdom that God was bringing to earth, one that would shatter all other kingdoms and last forever.

Survival Principle: The more oppressive the circumstances, the more crucial it is to maintain a vision of the ultimate victory.

Alexander the Great, Genghis Khan, Napoleon, Chairman Mao, and even Adolph Hitler were driven to success by visions of ultimate glory and victory. Christians are to be driven to survival and success by the promise of the perfect, invincible world order of Christ—the Kingdom of Christ.

Survival Principle: Life is threatening only for citizens of shaky kingdoms with insecure kings.

Once Daniel reckoned with the surety of the coming Rock that would smash the nations of the world and set up His own invincible world order, threats from the likes of Nebuchadnezzar, lions' dens, fiery furnaces, and evil conspirators faded. Daniel knew He was secure.

If you are tied to earthly structures, media dealmakers, contractual manipulators, market dynamics, or the ebb and flow of work, dollars, status, and favor, you'll need tranquilizers! All these are outcroppings of a shaky world order—the "kingdom of darkness"—which is destined for destruction. It's not *if*, but *when* it will collapse.

E. Stanley Jones tells of visiting Russia in the glory days of Communism. Workers carrying buckets of dirt out of tunnels for the Moscow subway were chanting, "We are building a better world." When hauling dirt is building a better world, you've still got the vision! You're a citizen of the Kingdom!

Survival Principle: Royalty is royalty—even in exile; never forget you are destined for the Kingdom.

LION'S DEN SURVIVAL PRINCIPLES, PART 23
How to Be Ten Times Better Than the Competition

"At the end of the time set by the king to bring them in, the chief official presented them to Nebuchadnezzar. The king talked with them, and he found none equal to Daniel, Hananiah, Mishael and Azariah, so they entered the king's service. In every matter of wisdom and understanding about which the king questioned them, he found them ten times better than all the magicians and enchanters in his whole kingdom."
— Daniel 1:18-20 (NIV)

It was a corporate climate in which "downsizing" was the dominant objective, and top executives of studios and networks were being dumped into the streets of Hollywood and New York by the hundreds. Still other execs were given "early retirement" or were having their contracts bought out in their fifties. In this environment, a Christian exec at a major TV network was given a three-year contract at age 70! How did this happen? Everybody inside and outside the network knew how valuable he was to the company—he was outstanding!

When Nebuchadnezzar looked over his new crop of graduates from Babylon's Officer Candidate School, four men stood above the rest. He perceived them as ten times better than the rest of the candidates. In view of their excellence, he overlooked the fact that they were Jewish aliens, slaves from Judah. He overlooked the fact that they had strange notions about everything from diet to deity. He could see what they could do for his kingdom.

All employers, like kings, want to recruit and keep really outstanding people. Many Christians in the often-hostile environment of media still have their jobs because there's nobody better to hire!

Survival Principle: There is no substitute for excellence; it is the path to success and high praise.

Proverbs 22:29 observes, "Do you see a man skilled in his work? He will serve before Kings. He will not serve before obscure men." You'll be passed over for more jobs—even in media—because you are mediocre than because you are a Christian.

"Well, yeah," you say, "But Daniel and the boys must have been blessed with exceptional talent. I'm not that gifted." It wasn't their talent that Nebuchadnezzar lauded. He was dazzled by their excellence in "every matter of wisdom and understanding." While their achievement no doubt required at least normal intelligence and some talent, wisdom and understanding are attributes largely distinct from both. My godly father grew up on a farm and never had a college course, but his wisdom and understanding were awesome. Wisdom and understanding can be acquired. [See the book of Proverbs.] Even those with modest gifts can share in them.

Survival Principle: Character and wisdom are acquired, not innate, and—in the long run—will overpower talent and charisma.

Finally, there is a powerful reminder in this passage about the insignificance of labels and titles. Did you note that in the list above the four are referred to by their Hebrew names, not their Babylonian ones! Nebuchadnezzar couldn't stand their Hebrew names, because they all glorified a god he didn't worship. So, he gave Daniel, Hananiah, Mishael and Azariah names honoring pagan deities—Belteshazzar, Shadrach, Meshach, and Abednego. After their God had shown His superior power through them, it didn't matter what they were called. They had the right stuff.

Powerful point. Bestowing titles or calling names doesn't change anybody's true character. Calling a person a "reverend" doesn't make him worthy of reverence—only character does that! Likewise, calling a person "self-righteous" shouldn't hinder his commitment to true righteousness.

Survival Principle: Don't be preoccupied with either titles or labels. It's better to be known by your character than your nomenclature.

LION'S DEN SURVIVAL PRINCIPLES, PART 24
No Story Is Complete Without an Ending

"At that time . . . there will be a time of distress such as has not happened from the beginning of nations until then. But at that time your people—everyone whose name is found written in the book—will be delivered. Multitudes who sleep in the dust of the earth will awake: some to everlasting life, others to shame and everlasting contempt. Those who are wise will shine like the brightness of the heavens, and those who lead many to righteousness like the stars . . . ."
— Daniel 12:1-3 (NIV)

Jean Paul Sartre, the French existentialist, wrote a monstrously depressing play entitled *No Exit* as the ultimate expression of his philosophy. Since Sartre believed that human life has no Planner and no Plan, he portrayed an eternity in which depressed and hopeless people get off an elevator into an endless existence in which they live for each moment in ultimate selfishness with . . . no exit. Depressing indeed! Yet, this philosophy of life is common in the often-vacuous world of the media.

In contrast to this worldview, Daniel—in the final vision given to him by God—heard the words of the Planner and saw the end of the Plan! The vision, a powerful presentation of God's philosophy of history, can be summed up in three statements. One, at the end time, things will get worse before they get better. Two, a general resurrection will take some people to eternal life and others to eternal shame, and, three, wise people should be spreading their spiritual light now.

Daniel's vision fits like a glove with that of The Revelation chapters 4-19 in predicting an end to life as we know it marked by unprecedented suffering and distress. The proverbial Four Horsemen of the Apocalypse are part of that vision as they bring oppression, bloodshed, economic collapse, famine, and disease. Thank God, the story doesn't end there.

God will then resurrect all those who "sleep in the dust of the earth" to face His decision about their future. Those whose names are "written in the book" are delivered from the final suffering to eternal blessing. Knowing this is powerful motivation for survival in whatever kind of distress we experience. Enduring the horrific ordeal of a shipwreck is easier if you know your name is on the rescue list, so be sure your name is written in the "Book of Life." (Revelation 20:11-15)

Survival Principle: Life is most precious when it is threatened. No distress, no deliverance.

The "eternal shame" part of Daniel's vision may not sound like good news to those who want to believe that everybody goes to heaven, that "all roads lead to the top of the mountain." But the absence of a hell is radically more depressing. It means that the Adolph Hitlers of the world go to the same place as do the Mother Theresas. It means there is no justice for evildoers. It means that the "How-could-a-loving-God-allow" questions go forever unanswered. Judgment and hell are wonderful motivators to goodness and belief. Take judgment and hell out of the future life and you introduce them into the present one.

Survival Principle: Trust in a God who can empower you to goodness and rescue you from hell, or you will end up with evildoers in this life and the next.

Jesus expressed the same concept as the Father did in part three of Daniel's revelation when He said, "Let your light so shine before men that they may see your good works and glorify your father who is in heaven." (Matthew 5:16) The message to Daniel declared that the "wise will shine . . . and lead many to righteousness." In a nation where 97% of Christians say they have never led another person to Jesus Christ in a one-on-one setting, and 90% say they have never gone through an entire presentation of the Gospel with an unbeliever, we have a lot of foolish believers.

Survival Principle: By spreading your light, you not only illumine your own path, you avoid responsibility for those in your social circle who fall in the darkness.

CONCLUSION
Getting Beyond Survival

A Confession. I gave this book the wrong name. Really.

I used the word "survival" in the title, and this never should have been done. I do not believe *for one nanosecond* that God ever intended for us—the members of His royal family—merely to *survive*. *Conquest* was all He ever had in mind for Kingdom citizens. If survival were God's goal, we would be worshipping the God of the Mediocre. We are not. We are worshipping the King of all Kings and the Lord of all Lords.

But, I left the title as it is, because I've observed that in order to *conquer* you first have to *survive* . . . and most people I meet are struggling somewhere slightly above the survival line. I heard about a guy whose family had chiseled on his tombstone, "He came here, he stayed here, and he left." Then, there was the poem I saw written in graffiti once on a college campus:

> I serve one purpose in this school on which no
> man can frown.

I quietly go to class each day and keep the average down.

Friend, get beyond the *survival* stage in your life. Become the enemy of the mediocre and the average in your life.

"Easy for you to say," you say. "You don't have my [fill in the blank] job, spouse, neighbor, health issues, financial problems, or . . .." True, I don't. And my challenges are unique to me as well. But, if you have a personal relationship with Jesus Christ, then we share the same infinite power to deal with our struggles.

I like saying, "I just realized that—between Bill Gates and me—we are worth more than fifty billion dollars." It reminds me that—between my Heavenly Father and me—we have enough resources to handle anything. So do you.

Years ago, I was a guest at a fabulous five star hotel in Cuernavaca Mexico. Trust me, staying there was not martyrdom. The hotel restaurant had global recognition for its cuisine, the rooms were lavishly decorated and spacious, and the formal gardens were suited to a palace. Touring the grounds the first day I arrived, I saw a wall with a wrought iron gate, and peered through it to discover an incredibly beautiful swimming pool surrounded by statuary and more lovely gardens. There were just a handful of people lounging around the pool, and I envied them a bit. I tried the handle on the gate, but it was locked.

In the days that I stayed there—enjoying the generosity of my hosts—I peered more than once through that wrought iron gate to enjoy the beauty of the pool and gardens. The crystal clear water in the pool looked so inviting in the muggy, tropical heat. But, no, it was locked.

At the day and time for checkout, I gathered my bags and surrendered them to the bellhop. On my way through the gardens to the lobby, I took one more look through that iron gate, fingering my room keys as I did. Did I say "keys"? Yes, there was a second, smaller key on the ring, one I had assumed was for the in-room mini-bar or something.

Looking at the gate, then the key, I had a burst of insight. Could it be? I placed that key in the lock, and it turned the tumblers. That lovely garden and pool were reserved for hotel guests. It was locked to keep non-paying visitors out. That entire stay, *I had had the key* to that fabulous area, and, now, in moments, I would have to give it back to the hotel without ever enjoying a special privilege reserved for *me*.

Amid the pressure, conflict, heartache, and hostility of life, God has prepared for us, His children, a lovely garden of the soul filled with the Water of Life and surrounded by the lush flora of the Spirit. Those who are not adoptees into the Royal Family are locked out. No key they possess will fit the lock.

Unfortunately, most of us have never tried the key . . . by never internalizing the timeless principles for both survival *and* conquest that have given men and women of faith over the millennia power to live as victors amid the warfare of life.

So, I leave you with one more principle:

Conquest Principle: Deploy all the resources of God at your disposal through full and constant surrender to Him, and a little bit of heaven will be yours long before you reach the real place.

APPENDIX
Just the Principles

1. You must have a clear definition of your moral nonnegotiables.

2. You must weigh the immediate cost of defending your righteous standards against the long-term cost of violating them.

3. Remember that your life is not your career; your life is your character and your quality relationships.

4. Whether you "make it" or not, life will go on.

5. Never curry favor. Trust God to grant or withdraw it.

6. Those who trust the Lord to give favor get ahead farther and faster. Those who curry favor are ultimately despised and ridiculed as weak, untrustworthy, and lacking in integrity.

7. Tend tiny, moral decisions. Your soul is not sold in one great auction; it is bartered away in thousands of tiny trades.

8. Seek your security in Christ. Security, for the Christian, is never based on what one can see; it is

founded on promises given by a loving, Heavenly Father.

9. Have a godly support group to go to for spiritual support and accountability.

10. Mobilize prayer, and then listen for the answer.

11. Don't confuse being unfulfilled or out of work with being out of commission. God hasn't forgotten you or abandoned His plans for you.

12. Maintain the kind of character and reputation that will recommend you when the "big job" comes along.

13. Make it clear that, when it comes to doing what's right, you can't be bought.

14. If your spiritual integrity can be bought at any price, the numbers are meaningless, and Satan will always make sure somebody is in the bidding.

15. What is done with the price offered for our integrity after we turn it down is God's business. In any case, He'll find a way to replace and multiply our reward for faithfulness.

16. Bosses are to be respected, but not feared, because they have no ultimate authority.

17. In matters of conscience, we must prayerfully prepare an open appeal to the authority, one that supports his objectives.

18. When faced with directives that violate your conscience, provide a creative solution that will enhance your boss's image and success . . . and protect your own integrity.

19. Tend well every area of your life and work. Not to do so gives your enemies an advantage.

20. Be willing to be viewed as a fanatic to pursue your relationship with God and practice your faith.

21. Those with spiritual authority in their lives never have to argue or defend themselves.

22. Those whose lives are built on the foundation of their faith in an all-powerful God are unshakable.

23. Count on the long-term rewards of obedience, even if the short-term situation goes against you.

24. Allow your human spirit or personality to be totally possessed and dominated by the Spirit of Christ.

25. Give God credit for all the good He does. To cop part of the credit is to ask to be humbled.

26. When all hell breaks loose, keep praying prayers of thanksgiving.

27. When you're going through the fire, you don't have to be in bondage to it.

28. Whether you can see Him or not, the Son of God is never closer to you than in your adversity. Count on it!

29. Respond in such a way in adversity that others can see the Son of God in you, whether you are consciously aware of His presence or not.

30. God doesn't mind our displaying the talents, skills, and successes in our lives, so long as we make it unmistakably clear that He is the source of them all.

31. There are few limits to how much success we can enjoy, if we don't care who gets the credit for it.

32. Exalt yourself, and God will demote you. Humble yourself before Him, and He will lift you up.

33. Believers in a hostile environment cannot "hole up" in some underground bunker as the war rages overhead. They must take up arms with the weapons of the Spirit and intercede on behalf of the collective war effort and even the sins of others.

34. When all hell breaks loose, don't fight it; call on heaven to handle it. In the long run, heaven can always handle hell!

35. In a crisis, one word from the Lord is better than ten thousand from anyone else.

36. Praise is the agent that stills the tempest in the hearts of believers, when God chooses not to still the tempest around them.

37. Hang in there until God finishes His work. Leaving one second before God brings victory is catastrophic; hanging around ten years after He does is sharing in the spoils.

38. Difficulty is not a reliable indicator of impending defeat, because it is also the typical setting in which victory is secured.

39. Difficulty is the environment for miracle, unless it is to be a very great miracle; then, the environment is impossibility.

40. Gain understanding. It is far more valuable than wealth, power, or prestige.

41. You learn nothing with your tongue loose; that's why it's one of the few organs God made with its own cage.

42. God ultimately doesn't bless the self-made man; he'll just worship his maker more fervently.

43. If you want God to speak well of you in times to come, you have to pursue His will and way today.

44. Don't be preoccupied with status. Pursue stature, and status—with God and man—will be your reward.

45. If you want God to hear your prayers, be sure you acknowledge and express that you don't deserve to be heard.

46. In prayer, remember to whom you are speaking, or God won't "remember" what you say.

47. Never ask God for what you deserve; that's asking for hell. You don't want justice! Beg for mercy.

48. Allowing exploitation to drive us deeper into trust is far superior to allowing it to drive us into bitterness.

49. God's defense of His faithful ones is far more effective and comprehensive than our feeble attempts to defend ourselves.

50. The more oppressive the circumstances, the more crucial it is to maintain a vision of the ultimate victory.

51. Life is threatening only for citizens of shaky kingdoms with insecure kings.

52. Royalty is royalty—even in exile; never forget you are destined for the Kingdom.

53. There is no substitute for excellence; it is the path to success and high praise.

54. Character and wisdom are acquired, not innate, and—in the long run—will overpower talent and charisma.

55. Don't be preoccupied with either titles or labels. It's better to be known by your character than your nomenclature.

56. Life is most precious when it is threatened. No distress, no deliverance.

57. Trust in a God who can empower you to goodness and rescue you from hell, or you will end up with evildoers in this life and the next.

58. By spreading your light, you not only illumine your own path, you avoid responsibility for those in your social circle who fall in the darkness.

59. <u>Conquest Principle</u>: Deploy all the resources of God at your disposal through full and constant surrender to Him, and a little bit of heaven will be yours long before you reach the real place.